VOU

VISUAL POETRY, TOKIO, 1958–1978

vou

VISUAL POETRY, TOKIO, 1958–1987

edited by Taylor Mignon

introduction by Eric Selland

ISOBAR
PRESS

Published in 2022 by

Isobar Press
Sakura 2-21-23-202, Setagaya-ku,
Tokyo 156-0053, Japan

&

14 Isokon Flats, Lawn Road,
London NW3 2XD, United Kingdom

https://isobarpress.com

ISBN 978-4-907359-38-6

ACKNOWLEDGEMENTS AND PUBLISHER'S NOTE

With grateful thanks to Hashimoto Sumiko for permission to reproduce the photographs of VOU Club members on the back cover and on pages 15 and 112, as well as material from the covers designed by Kitasono Katue for the following issues of *VOU* magazine: 61, 77, 97, 100, 110, 112, 118, 122, 130, 132, 152, 153, and 154. Many thanks also to all the poets for permission to reproduce their work; in two cases, in spite of every effort having been made, we were unable to contact the poet or find a copyright holder.

In this book Japanese names appear in the Japanese order, with the family name first.

This publication is dedicated to the memory of

Karl Young (1947–2017)

Coeditor

VOU

REVUE

DE

LA POESIE ACTUELLE

numero 61

VOU CLUB

CONTENTS

INTRODUCTION

This long-overdue publication fills a gap in the understanding of postwar Japanese poetry and the role of visual poetry in the avant-garde of Japan's postwar period. It is a highly welcome book. The VOU Club was a group of outsider poet-artists with their roots in Japan's Modernist avant-garde of the 1930s who were an active part of Japan's tumultuous 1960s and 1970s. This was a time of political unrest due to the populist reaction against the security pact between the U.S. and Japan, as well as antiwar sentiments held by students and leftist thinkers and artists. It was also a very active time for underground theater by the likes of Terayama Shuji, who encouraged young people to drop out of mainstream society and live an alternative lifestyle rather than work for Japan's conservative corporations. However, as time went on, the activities of the group faded into the past. VOU poets failed to gain the official recognition of Japan's conservative poetry community. The work has been kept alive and documented by a small group of poets and scholars, themselves 'outsiders' of a sort. Here, for the first time, a selection of VOU visual poetry is made available in print.

VOU visual poetry has its roots in the work of poet Kitasono Katue.[1] Kitasono was originally an artist and designer who became involved in Modernist and avant-garde poetry magazines in Tokyo in the 1920s, when new experimental poetry and arts blossomed after the great earthquake of 1923. The city itself was newly rebuilt and this was a factor in the excitement of the new and the modern. Kitasono was involved in Surrealism and Dadaism and established the VOU Club in 1935 in order to bring artists and poets interested in these movements together. Around that same time, he began an intensive correspondence with Ezra Pound. Throughout his career Kitasono had many international contacts, such as Haroldo de Campos of the concrete poetry movement in the 1950s. James Laughlin of New Directions and poet Kenneth Rexroth were also in contact with Kitasono and were aware of VOU's avant-garde activities, including some of the VOU poets in their international annual a number of times during the 1970s, but this seems not to have stuck in the American consciousness during a period in which American poets were more interested in Zen and haiku.

The Modernist period was one in which the materiality of language became an element of growing interest, with poets making use of that awareness and the openness to new forms in a wide variety of ways, but most never wandering too far from language's semantic foundations. But some poets did venture into visual poetry following

---

[1] The spelling of Kitasono's name uses non-standard romanization, which was Kitasono's own preference. John Solt, *Shredding the Tapestry of Meaning: The Poetry and Poetics of Kitasono Katue (1902-1978)*, Harvard University Asia Center, 1999.

Apollinaire who was one of the earliest poets to focus on the visual elements of poetry. Though Japanese Dadaist poet, Hagiwara Kyōjirō, experimented with such visual elements, Kitasono was the first to venture further in the direction of total abstraction, eventually cutting ties completely with the semantic foundations of language. His roots as a visual artist may have been one of the factors making this possible, but Karl Young,[2] who curated a major selection of Japanese visual poetry on the internet, stated in his lengthy introduction that he felt strongly that there is something in Japanese culture and history providing Japanese poets with a sensibility that leans more naturally toward visual poetry than does the Western concept of language. Young did not pursue this question further, so we are left somewhat up in the air. However, he may have been onto something, and it is not the usual mistaken assumption about the pictorial quality of Chinese characters.[3] (In fact, according to John Solt, Kitasono's biographer, the avoidance of Japanese written characters in his works as he began to distance himself from the concrete poetry movement was because of the Western tendency to exoticize Chinese characters.)

Writing has long appeared in painting in the Japanese tradition, such that it is a part of the painting rather than outside commentary. The written symbol can also be used to decorate objects of daily use such as tea cups and so on. In the art of calligraphy, words and phrases are written in a highly stylized manner such that meaning is often not immediately discernable. The characters can at the same time be appreciated as abstract images. The viewer knows that they have meaning, but that meaning may merely be hinted at. This ability to appreciate writing as art without demanding a meaning or logic, in other words without a utilitarian function, may be something that naturally lends itself to the production of visual poetry. But this doesn't explain VOU's venture into completely non-semantic terrain, or Japanese mainstream poetry's tendency to ignore their importance.

The significance of postwar VOU visual poetry is that dependence on semantic relationships (or ideogrammatic relationships) has been broken, moving the art more into the area of total abstraction. To place the artists included in this collection into the context of their own times we have to look at events following WWII. The

---

[2] Karl Young, to whose memory this anthology is dedicated, was an important progenitor of the American avant-garde during the 1960s and 70s and one of the first to introduce computer-based poetry. He also gave encouragement and support to the Language poets when they were getting started. Unfortunately, his contributions have been all but forgotten due to his own modesty and the tragic loss of his personal archive not long before his death.

[3] Current scholarship classifies Chinese characters as being a logographic writing system, a complex system using both sound and meaning. Many characters are compounds made up of parts of other characters based on their meanings. There are of course a small number of characters with pictographic or ideographic origins, but that is not how the system works.

complete destruction of not only Japan's cities and industry, but the total collapse of a particular world-view and identity, had wiped the slate clean, and writers and artists felt that they could start over like new. Many reveled in their new-found freedom, but there were intellectual and philosophical gaps that needed to be filled, such as the problem of identity. What did it mean to be Japanese after the collapse of the Japanese empire? These issues were taken up by a new group of writers producing what became known as *Nikutai Bungaku,*[4] which expressed the sense that the only identity possible for a person to adopt after the total destruction of Japan was the body and sexuality. This plays out in various ways in literature, film, and performance (Butoh for instance). One major interest was eroticism in art and writing. It was both an expression of freedom and a search for identity. In the 1960s this interest in eroticism continues, but in the Vietnam war and anti-ANPO protest era, it takes an especially violent aspect.[5] This can be seen in some of the more controversial VOU works and also in the major photographers of the time, as well as in the experimental theater of Terayama Shuji. In the introduction to his study of Terayama, Steven C. Ridgely writes that 'a broad trend of eroticized violation narratives emerges in Vietnam-era Japan.'[6] This is seen in the work of Mishima, Oe, and the critic Shibusawa who translated the works of Sade. We can also see this tendency in some of the work included in this selection, especially that of Okazaki.

Perhaps one of the fascinating things about the work of the VOU group overall is that the pieces range from the highly physicalized and eroticized to work that reflects a kind of absolute abstraction. One wonders how something like this could fall so easily by the wayside. For one thing, VOU's founder, Kitasono Katue, had become *persona non grata* in mainstream poetry circles due to his failure to publicly show repentance for what leftist critic, Yoshimoto Takaaki, saw as collaboration with the militarist authorities during the war.[7] Kitasono felt that he had nothing to apologize for, and continued his avant-garde activities as before, but this had to be done completely outside any of the mainstream poetry circles. VOU's place in the Japanese arts of the 1960s was as a kind of *angura* (a term usually referring to the underground theater[8] of the time,

---

[4] See *The Body in Postwar Japanese Fiction,* by Douglas N. Slaymaker, Routledge (2004), as well as other books covering this subject in the bibliography.

[5] ANPO is the Japanese term for the US–Japan Security Treaty, originally signed in 1952. The revision of the treaty in 1960 triggered massive protests, often turning violent. There was a repeat of this situation in 1970.

[6] Steven C. Ridgely, *Japanese Counterculture: The Antiestablishment Art of Terayama Shuji.* University of Minnesota Press (2011), p. xxv.

[7] John Solt covers this part of Kitasono's past in great detail in *Shredding the Tapestry of Meaning.*

[8] See Ridgely, *Japanese Counterculture: The Antiestablishment Art of Terayama Shuji.*

but it can also be used for non-mainstream activities in general). As time went on and other issues were uppermost in the minds of poets, VOU still had difficulty getting the attention of the mainstream poetry community due to a problem shared by visual poetry everywhere.[9] This is the difficulty of reconciling the differing interpretations of visual poetry: is it poetry materializing itself as object or non-linguistic image, or is it simply visual art since, after all, it no longer makes use of language as its main means of expression?

There is one more possible reason for this falling by the wayside of the VOU Club's work, but this is only an educated guess based on my own involvements with Japanese poetry during the 1980s: it is that perhaps Kitasono and his group were simply too international, going over the heads of the local poetry community and directly to European groups. This would have made them somehow inauthentic as Japanese poets. During the early, chaotic years of postwar Japanese poetry, questions of identity remained fairly open, but gradually, as the new postwar canon began to form, concerns began to gather around the forming of a uniquely Japanese identity – one that of course rejected the extremes of the war period, but which tended to canonize poets in whom some kind of unique or authentic Japaneseness could be seen. The icons of modern Japanese poetry during the postwar period were Hagiwara Sakutaro and Nakahara Chuya, poets who were part of the avant-garde in their own, prewar time; but now the interpretation of their work began to gather around the lyric beauty of their poetry and other elements of their lives and work deemed uniquely Japanese. The more difficult and experimental aspects of their activities were brushed to the side. A certain range of experimentation was tolerated by the postwar canon as long as it did not go beyond certain limits, but even the linguistic-based poems of Kitasono and his group tended to go beyond those limits. Moreover, Kitasono's use of humor was thought to be a sign of a lack of the seriousness felt to be appropriate for an authentically Japanese lyric self.

The work included in this selection has been cared for and preserved by Taylor Mignon and a handful of other people without whose efforts it would have fallen into oblivion. It is hoped that this publication will bring about more awareness of Japan's dynamic experimental tradition in poetry during the twentieth century and encourage further study and research.

Eric Selland
Tokyo, November 7, 2021

[9] Willard Bohn discusses the various arguments surrounding visual poetry in his publication, *The Aesthetics of Visual Poetry: 1914-1928*, The University of Chicago Press (1986).

vou

REVUE DE LA POESIE EXPERIMENTALE

NUMERO 115

vou

REVUE DE LA POESIE EXPERIMENTALE

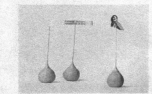

NUMERO 115

vou

NUMERO 115

VOU
VOU

NUMERO 125

vou

NUMERO 125

SHIMIZU Toshihiko SHIMAMURA ry e SAWADA shinichi MARI natsuo INOUE mitsuko NANO yoshiro KO DA tatsuya UNO kei TORII shuzo TSUJI setsuko julien BLAINE KIYO HARA atsushi TAKAHASHI shohio hiro FUKUDA kazuhiko OKAZAKI katsuhiko BAN naoko JINBO ke isuke TERAYAMA chiyoko SUZUKI takoshi ITO isao

vou

NUMERO 126

AVRIL

1976

TAKAHASHI Shohachiro · UNO Toknihi · TORII Shuzo · BAN Naoko · M ARI Natsuo · NANO Yoshiro · SHIMIZU Toshihiko · TSUKATANI Akihiro · ISHII Motoko · ITO Motoyuki · SAWADA Shin'ichi · OKAZAKI Katsuhiko · Julien BLAINE · SARENCO · KIYOHARA Etsushi · FUKUDA Kazuhiko · TSUJI Setsuko · JINBO Keisuke · ITO Isao · KITASONO Katue

v
o
u

NUMERO 127
SEPTEMBRE
1976

REVUE DE LA POESIE EXPERIMENTALE

ITO Isao · TSUJI Setsuko · FUKUDA Kazuhiko · SHIMIZU Toshihiko · MORIMOTO Hidekazu · TABEI Takeshi · WAKABAYASHI Mitsuo · OKAZAKI Katsuhiko · SAWADA Shin'ichi · KIYOHARA Etsushi · SEKI Shiro · HIBINO Fumiko · TORII Ryozan · KIDA Tatsuya · TABEI BAN Koki · YODA Toshiharu · SARENCO · SHIMIZU Sherato · SUZUKI Takeshi · NANO Yoshiro

v
o
u

NUMERO 150
NOVEMBRE
1976

REVUE DE LA POESIE EXPERIMENTALE

TSUJI Setsuko · FUKUDA Kazuhiko · JINBO Keisuke · TAMURA Koh · YODA Toshiharu · TORII Shuzo · KITASONO Katué · SHIMIZU Toshihiko · MORIMOTO Hidekazu · KIBINO Fumiko · KIYOHARA Etsushi · SEKI Shiro · OKAZAKI Katsuhiko · TORII Ryozan · Julien BLAINE · ITO Isao · TABEI Takeshi · FUNAKI Hitoshi · WAKABAYASHI Mitsuo · NANO Yoshiro

v
o
u

NUMERO 169
FEVRIER
1978

REVUE DE LA POESIE EXPERIMENTALE

ITO Isao · TSUJI Setsuko · FUKUDA Kazuhiko · SHIMIZU Toshihiko · FUNAKI Hitoshi · KIDA Tatsuya · MORIMOTO Hidekazu · SEKI Shiro · KUSAKAI Toshio · YODA Toshiharu · Pierre GARNIER · SAWADA Shin'ichi · TORII Ryozan · OKAZAKI Katsuhiko · Ernest BUCHWALD · KIYOHARA Etsushi · HIBINO Fumiko · JINBO Keisuke · TAMURA Koh · TORII Shuzo · TABEI Takeshi · SHIMAMURA Ryo · NANO Yoshiro · OKUNABI Tetsuo · WARABAYASHI Mitsuo · TERAYAMA Chiyoko · SUZUKI Takeshi

30th EXHIBITION VISUAL ACTIVITIES • VOU GROUP
KINOKUNIYA GALLERY • AUGUST 22–27 • TOKIO

from left to right:

(Names of members featured in this anthology are printed in blue.)

TSUKUTANI Akihiro

NARAYAMA Fujio

SEKI Shiro (TANABE Shin)

TSUJI Setsuko

FUKUDA Kazuhiko

SHIMIZU Toshihiko

KITASONO Katue

Mrs OKAZAKI

YODA Yoshiharu

SHIMIZU Masato

FUJITA Kohei

KIYOHARA Etsushi

HIBINO Fumiko

OKAZAKI Katsuhiko

Not pictured:

ITŌ Motoyuki, SAWADA Shin'ichi, TAKAHASHI Shōhachirō

TSUJI Setsuko

Tsuji Setsuko (Sugiyama Hisako, 1927–1993) was, according to John Solt, one of the most 'uncompromising and dedicated contemporary avant-garde photographers in Japan.' Her lexical and visual poetry, composed in a strongly surrealist style, show the influence of her mentor Kitasono Katue, yet express distinctive viewpoints. Before joining the VOU Club, she was a member of the coterie associated with the magazine *Pan Poesie,* and after VOU, published her own journal *0,* some images from which are included here. Her visual poetry, created with a camera, was published in the U.S. in *New Directions in Poetry and Prose 34* in 1977 and her poem 'Sand's Design / Poem,' translated by John Solt, was published in 1988 in a special section on VOU poets in the magazine *Third Rail.* Her work also appeared in *Cold Drill* in 1991. She published twelve volumes of poetry, a poetry chapbook, a collection of short stories and a collection of visual poetry.

If the catchphrase of surrealism is 'as beautiful as the chance encounter of a sewing machine and an umbrella on an operating table,' Tsuji's might be 'as elegant as a sandal-legged keyhole below a Panama hat.' Traditionally, the combination of such concrete particulars was utilized in the practice of haiku composition. Poet and critic Nishiwaki Junzaburo (1894–1982) argued that lines written by Matsuo Bashō (1644–1694) were precursors to European surrealism in their joining of contrasting elements – although that contention does not seem to be widely acknowledged by critics of literary modernism. A perhaps more fitting analogy for Tsuji's work (albeit in a different genre) would be that of experimental poet Yamamura Bochō (1884–1924), who wrote the poem 'Geigo' (literally, delirious speech) in 1913. This poem contains crime-related nouns on one side of the page with nouns from random categories on the other side – *abduction sponge-cake, robbery trumpet, blackmail sitar, gambling cat,* for example (translation by Miryam Sas). Thus, before the founding of Europe-based surrealism, there was already pioneering work of a highly surrealist nature in Japan. Tsuji's 'plastic poems' here show the carrying-over of juxtaposition from the haiku tradition into a purely visual presentation, away from its lexical foundation.

Tsuji often portrayed the human form, using a variety of everyday media, and placing her figures in unexpected contexts. In *op. 016,* between two rectangular sections of corrugated cardboard, a cowboy looks away from the viewer. Above the cowboy, the head of a philosopher-like personage peeks from the top of the cardboard, to ponderous, poetic and humorous effect. In haiku, or more precisely, in the *senryu* form (where the human rather than the natural is central), I suggest it could be interpreted as 'a philosopher peeks from above corrugated cardboard at a cowboy contemplating the void.' Tsuji's works combine the profundity of haiku with the surreal randomness of Yamamura's 'Geigo' to create her own elegant and nuanced visual idiom.

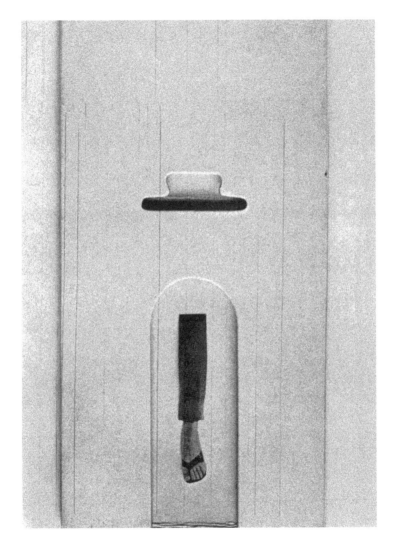

high summer

Photo poem

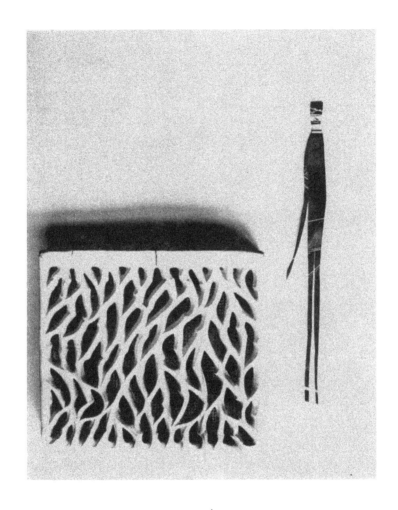

op. 4

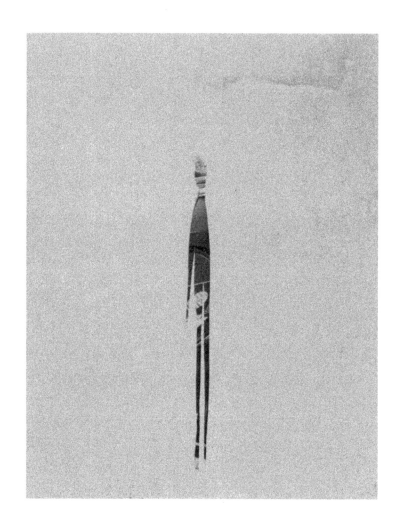

op. 5

op. 5

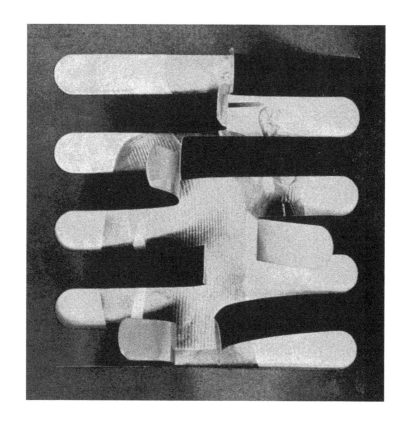

op 77-1

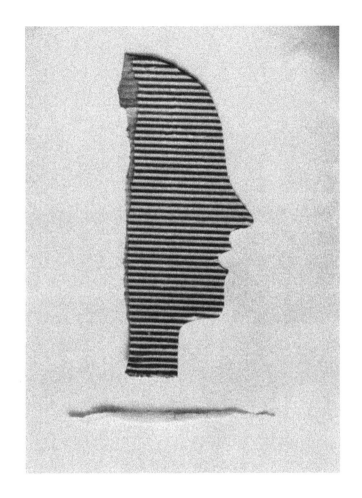

opus I

op. I

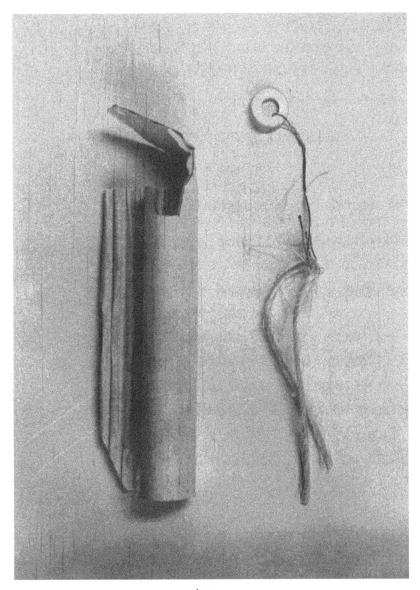

drome

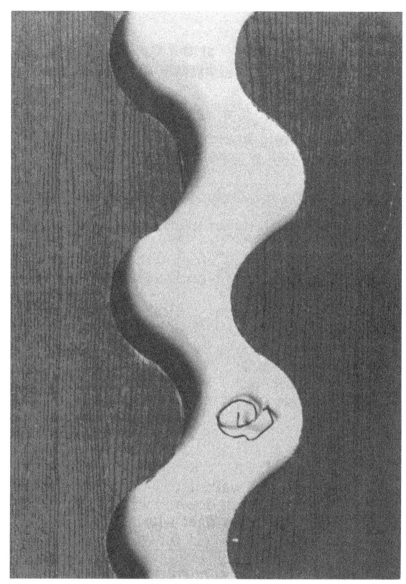

op. 001 or 川のある記憶　*(memory with river)*

two people eating the moon

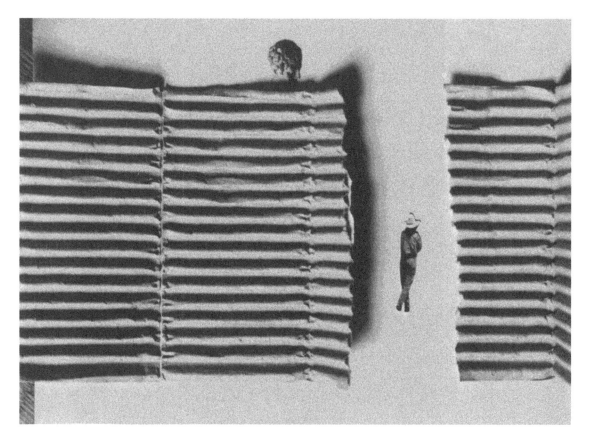

op. 016

op. 017

SHIMIZU Toshihiko

Shimizu Toshihiko (1929–2007) was born in Chiba prefecture and studied in the science department of the University of Tokyo before going on to graduate from the literature department of Gakushuin, another leading Tokyo university. He was a poet, jazz critic, and art critic. In addition to publishing in *VOU*, Shimizu's work appeared in the journals *Shigaku* (Poetics), *Gendaishitecho* (Handbook of Contemporary Poetry) and *Mugen* (Infinity). In 1988 he published a volume of poetry, *Chokuritsu enjin* (Upright Monkey), and among his books of jazz criticism are *Jazz Avant-Garde Chronicle 1967–1989, Jazu noto* (Jazz Notes) and *Jazz Alternative*; he also contributed an article to the anthology *Shōwa jazu-ron shūsei* (Shōwa Jazz Theory Collection). He wrote the liner notes for the Japanese version of John Zorn's *Spy vs. Spy: The Music of Ornette Coleman* and Sun Ra Arkestra's *Live from Soundscape,* among many other albums. He cowrote lyrics for one of the songs on the Otomo Yoshihide album *Invisible Songs – Sora*, with Brigitte Fontaine, and his collages graced the covers of albums by the Steve Lacy Sextet and the Masahiko Togashi Trio.

Many VOU poet-artists who published in the photographic section of the journal followed the lead of its editor and eschewed the use of Japanese written characters, instead opting for incorporating roman letters, especially in French and English. They may have used these roman letters because of their exoticism – thus reversing Western poets' fascination with the 'oriental' ideogram – or perhaps Kitasono and the other VOU poet-artists genuinely admired roman letters. Shimizu, in contrast, flew his Japanese-character flag proudly. He peppered many of his visual works not only with French and English, but with kanji, katakana and hiragana (all in one work), at times the characters being upside down, skewed or made vague by being placed on a dark background, as in *variation*. With the ideograms for 'rain' and 'ghost' and the arbitrary juxtapositions of images, such as that of a fish seemingly suspended in air, Picasso's 1954 *Portrait of Sylvette David in a Green Chair*, and a formally suited René Magritte-style man, the impression is one of discombobulation. In this work, the artist fuses together his concerns as jazz critic and art critic: the words 'Jazz By' can be seen and just below that, in katakana, a segment of the word 'piano'. Upside down in English, snippets of the words 'Europe,' 'Surrealism' and 'Dada' can be seen, even if the viewer-readers must complete the readings for themselves. The mystery, darkness and interpretative ambiguities of this method of collage composition evoke a key aesthetic concept of haiku called *yūgen*, which can be translated as 'profound subtlety,' or 'mystery and depth,' and which can be further extended to mean 'dark and obscure' or 'depth, density and distance' (Jeffrey Johnson). Shimizu's way of working with densely compacted fragments of printed script is seen at its most intense in his 1965 works *text picture, letter picture a2,* and *letter picture b1*, magnified details of two of which can be seen inside the front covers of this book.

high noon

text picture

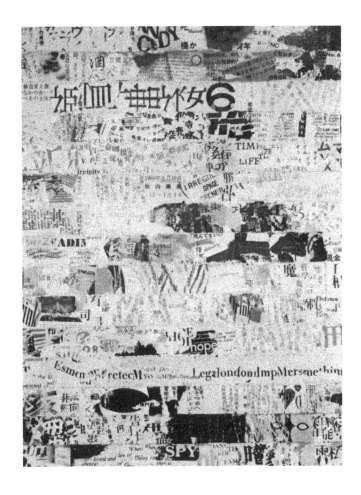

letter picture A2

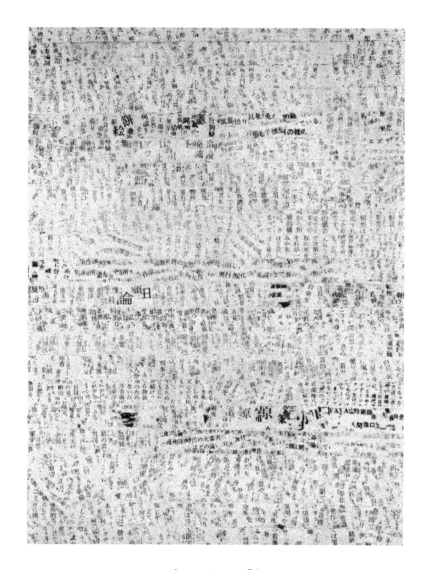

letter picture B1

hommage a augusto de campos: popcrete poem 1968

言 (word, say) – 詩 (poetry) – 寺 (temple)

variation

op. 691

sculpture in environment

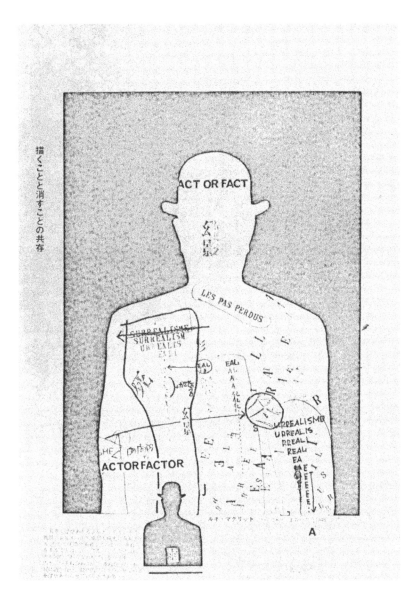

anti-illusion 1

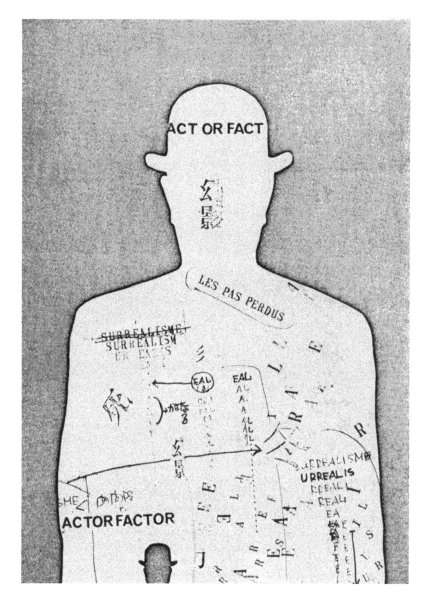

anti-illusion 2

a square of sky cut by the size of my head
ぼくの頭の大きさに切り取られた空の四角

postcard event / sky

ITŌ Motoyuki

Born in Kitakami, Iwate, in the north of Japan, Itō Motoyuki (1935–2020) was a friend of Takahashi Shōhachirō (see page 86), a fellow *VOU* poet born in the same town; the two poets often collaborated over the course of half a century. Itō participated in the avant-garde art group Group N39, published his visual poetry collection *Ear Festival* in 1971, and launched the visual poetry magazine *317* in 1975 with Shimizu Toshihiko (see page 30) and others. He was invited to exhibit at international exhibitions in Italy and the US, notably at the *Plastic Poems of Japan* exhibit at the Rhode Island School of Design in 1986–87. In 2007, along with Takahashi and experimental poet Fujitomi Yasuo, he played a lively part in *Playing Poetry: Performance Poetry*, an event in his hometown Kitakami. In the documentary film recording that event Itō is quoted as saying, 'A good point about poetry is that it can make you laugh. Going to poetry reading after poetry reading is boring unless the poet makes it humorous and engaging.'

Poet Kido Shuri tells an anecdote that captures how Itō wittily provokes thought through his visual poems: 'I received a postcard from Itō Motoyuki. For a moment, I thought it was just an ordinary postcard, but "word" and "world" were printed on it so that they canceled each other out or blended with each other. Was this a visual poem by Itō? The spread of meaning that arises from a slight difference in one word of the letter "l"! Imagine the world in words and search for words that compete with the world in the world created by words. The gift stunned me, but it was as if a single piece of paper was telling us that poetry is completely free-of-charge and nothing more than a gamble.'

Many of Itō's works either appeal to synesthesia or contemplate perceptions or paradoxes much like those of Buddhist koan. *ear festival a* obviously evokes synesthesia as the title refers to sound even though this is a visual poem. With the ideograms for 'ear' (耳), 'nest' (巣), and 'fruit' (果) placed among collaged images of birds, mummified bodies and a mastodon, the effect is visually powerful. Add to that the way separate shapes made of repeated single characters cluster together in clouds or swarms, and movement is implied – especially in the case of the hiragana character く in the top right segment of the piece, where the repeated character resembles a flock of birds. The characters 耳, 巣, and 果 are pronounced *mimi, su* and *ka* respectively, while the hiragana character く is pronounced *ku*. Sounded out loud, these flights of visual characters swarm in chattering flocks around the silence of the mummified bodies – a transient ear festival for an audience beyond hearing – with, in the background, possibly a faint suggestion that the birds might be about to devour the dead bodies in a version of sky burial.

inversion c

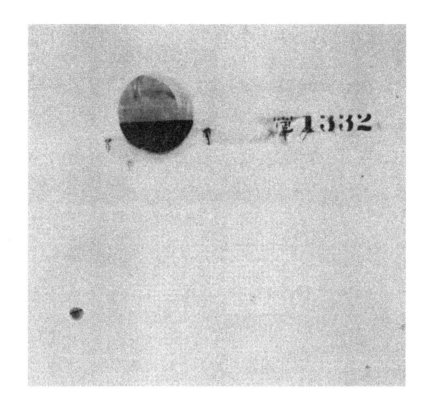

inversion d

inversion e

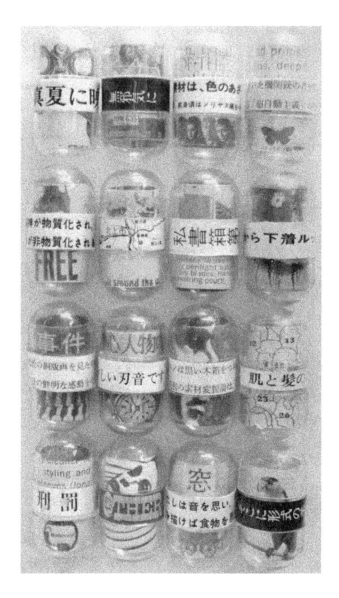

capsule plan 3

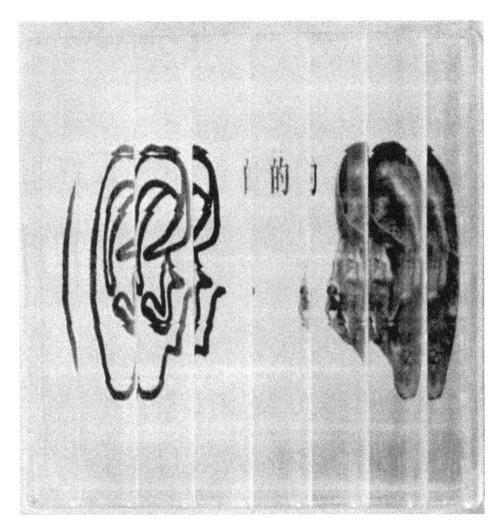

plastic poem 11

耳の祭 a (ear festival a)

耳の祭 b (ear festival b)

耳の祭 c (ear festival c)

OKAZAKI Katsuhiko

Okazaki Katsuhiko (1929–?), born in Nagoya, was a colorful character who grew up as the son of a yakuza boss. It is likely he died around 2006, when I stopped receiving New Year's cards from him. Okazaki was one of the leading avant-garde photographers in Japan; the subject matter of his photos is often erotic, and so his work can be seen as a precursor to that of the more famous Araki Nobuyoshi, even though Okazaki mostly avoided the mode of bondage that was Araki's specialty; when Okazaki does portray bondage, as in ♀ *and* ♀ on the facing page, it has a more playful, kitsch, and *fin-de-siècle* quality than Araki's very overt work. Okazaki published many photographic works in *VOU* from the 1950s on, and later, in the 1960s, published his photographic book *Lesbian Love* (1969) and held exhibitions at Tokyo art galleries. It is rumored that, later in life, his impassioned young wife burned all his photos, negatives, and his books, including *Lesbian Love*.

John Solt, the leading English-language scholar of the Japanese avant-garde, writes that 'the key to Okazaki's esthetic – and here he differed from his VOU colleagues – was that for him photography was defecation, vomiting, a literal expunging from the self's body (politic) through the lens by means of pressing the shutter. That said, his photos also show balanced compositions and superimpositions that double-expose an underlying orthodoxy. In my opinion, even when Okazaki is trying to show the ugly, it comes out quite beautiful … because, as ever, it's about the eye of the beholder' (personal communication by email, Aug 26, 2021).

There is an expectation that visual artists should produce aesthetically pleasing objects, but we cannot deny the importance of, for example, Luis Buñuel and Salvador Dali's film *Un Chien Andalou*, with the powerful surrealist shock created by its cutting of an eyeball, or even Méret Oppenheim's object *Fur Breakfast*; works like these remind us that art is also meant to disturb. Some of Okazaki's works, whether grotesque in style, such as *chaos* or *lovely vomit 4*, or else nakedly erotic, are clearly not intended to be soothing. However, although Okazaki was not deeply involved in the gentler esthetic of his VOU colleagues producing work in the plastic poem mode, he did occasionally produce works in that style, such as *requiem to A* and *requiem to Z*. Karl Young suggested in an unpublished article that 'visual poetry has ancient origins … beginning with "read-only" texts such as the configurations of stars in the night sky, the tracks of birds and animals, the patterns wind makes in grass, leaves, and water'; in *requiem to A* the overlapping capitalized As are behemoth constructs of man who has no right to fly among a flock of birds, the original poetic motion. Okazaki, while mostly producing works in an erotic, or erotically estranged, mode, in his *requiem* pieces showed he could be as poetically sophisticated as any of his VOU colleagues.

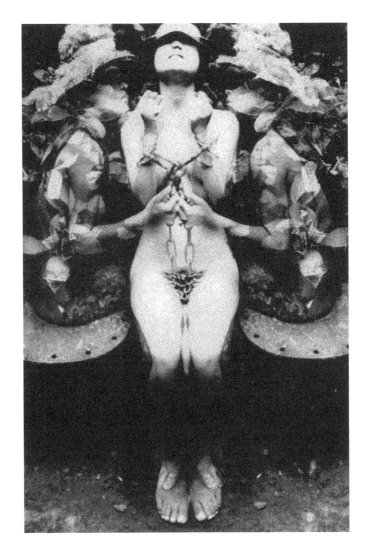

♀ and ♀

summer letter 1

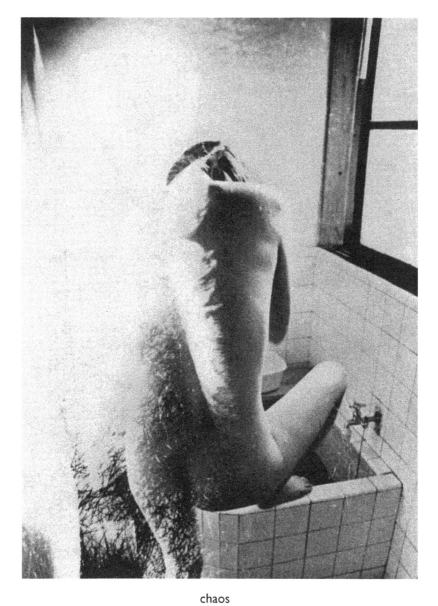

chaos

lovely vomit 4

adam & eve

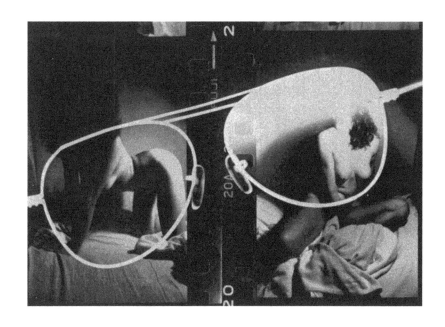

poemgraphy 3

poemgraphy <requiem to A>

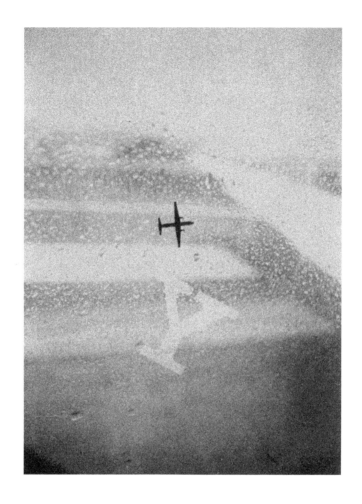

poemgraphy: requiem by the rain

poemgraphy <requiem to Z>

KIYOHARA Etsushi

Graphic artist and book designer Kiyohara Etsushi (1931–1988) was born in Tokyo. He graduated from the Department of Arts in the Faculty of Education at Tokyo University of Education (currently the University of Tsukuba) in 1955; a year later, in March 1956, he obtained a further degree from the same institution. He went on to found the Kiyohara Design Office, Ltd. He excelled as a typographer and book designer; among a number of important projects, he was responsible for the design of *The Drama of Terayama Shuji* (Shichosha, 1969–71), a collection of the dramatic work of the important avant-garde writer, playwright and film director. In addition, he translated *Le surréalism et l'après-guerre* by Tristan Tzara and designed the edition of this work published by Shichosha in 1971, and in 1974, along with Okamoto Tarō, and fellow *VOU* visual poet Fukuda Kazuhiko, contributed to a major work on the *shunga* (erotic art) of the Edo-period ukiyo-e artist Utagawa Kuniyoshi. He designed several books on Kitasono Katue and *VOU*, as well as Shimizu Toshihiko's book of poems *Upright Monkey* (see the profile of Shimizu on page 30).

Kiyohara practiced an astonishing array of styles of visual poetry, a credit to his expertise in graphic art and book design, which dovetailed with his role as a visual artist. There is, for example, the 'rock-stacking art' of *op. 6001*, as if someone were stacking stones beside a river; or, alternatively, levitating stones and rocks stacked horizontally rather than vertically, as in *composition e*, which could be called the 'sideways top-hat' style; in these works the simple rock shapes hover elegantly and elementally. Another approach is mostly linear, consisting of either straight or curving lines, with *op.–70–A–018*, for example, suggesting the trunks of a grove of bamboo. A further variation is the all-out collage style of *op. 1*, mixing phrases, magnifying letters (in this case the letter B), and combining a star-burst of cut-up language with graph-like layout and abstract figures to overwhelming yet subtle effect. There are the flying Rubik's Cube-like objects shooting off into the ether as in *op.–75–A–151*, which was the work used for the cover of the *New Directions 34* annual. In *op.–74–A–79* Rorschach blots and calligraphy are combined for a psychedelic effect, while *op.–76–A–160* calls to mind Sam Francis getting down to science.

Because of his wide range, it is impossible to ascribe one specific style to Kiyohara's work: this eclecticism, a testament to his being a distinguished graphic and book designer, allowed him to become one of the most prolific and professional of the visual poets featured here.

op. 6001

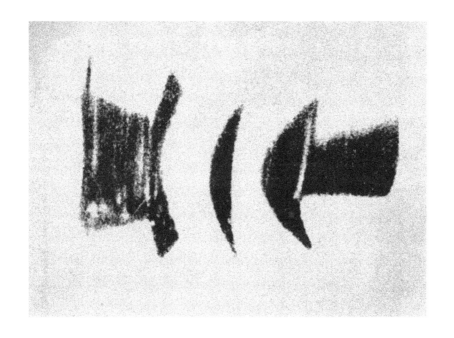

composition e

op. I

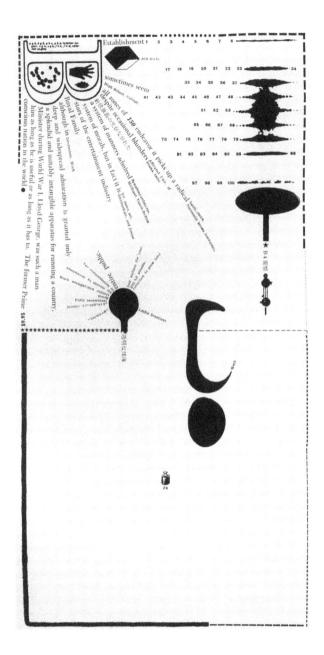

sometimes seem all zones of *150* endeavor it picks up a radical despite occasional blunders a system of morals, but in fact it is a system of manners admired stars of the entertainment industry. Royal Family although in amateurs, with deep and widespread admiration is granted only a splendid and suitably intangible apparatus for running a country. Minister during World War I, Lloyd George, was such a man him as long as he is useful or as long as it has to. The former Prime conscious nation in the world ●

Establishment 1 2 3 4 5 6 7 8

AIR MAIL

17 18 19 20 21 22 23 — 24
33 34 35 36 37
41 42 43 44 45 46 47 48
51 52 53
65 66 67 68
73 74 75 76 77 78 79
81 82 83 84 85 86 — 80

97 98 99 100

op. –70–A–018

op. −74−A−79

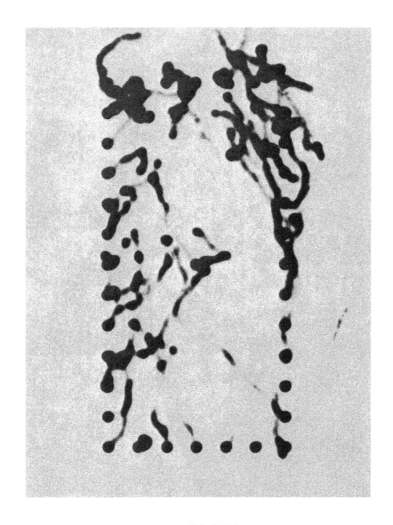

op. –74–A–80

op. –75–A–151

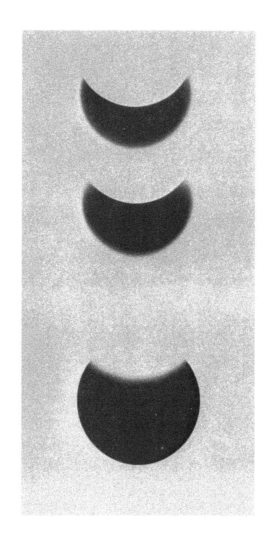

op. –76–A–153

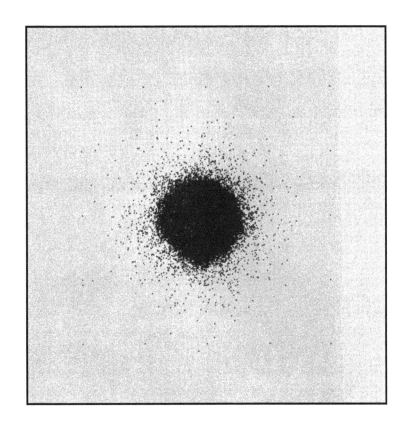

op. −76−A−160

SAWADA Shin'ichi

Most poetry journals in Japan contain no biographies of contributors. As a result, very little is known about Sawada Shin'ichi, other than the fact that he lived in Akabane in northwest Tokyo, close to the Arakawa River bordering Saitama Prefecture. There is only one mention of him on the internet. After *VOU* he was mostly published in δ (*Delta*) edited by Tanabe Shin, or in *O*, edited by Tsuji Setsuko. (For more information on these magazines, see the editor's afterword at the end of this volume.)

Sawada, like Okazaki Katsuhiko, was interested in representing the female form, but the two artists do this in very different ways and evoke a very different atmosphere. In Sawada's woman-centered work, the body parts are often juxtaposed in jarring ellipses. *generous time 1*, for example, shows a woman suntanning, with a block of seemingly random numbers fit between her left ear and left eye. Disquietingly, however, the elongated face is positioned higher than it should be, leaving the viewer to speculate what comprises the missing part of her face under the square of numbers. *generous time 2,* on the other hand, elegantly shows an enormous eye and below that, where the torso should be, the top part of a cascade of numbers aligned in meticulous numerical order. Below this is the lower body and the underwear, with the numbers plumed to either side of the legs. *generous time 1* is like glitch photography, as if the camera has broken, combining two disparate images, while *generous time 2* evokes the impulse of *cadavre exquis*, the French surrrealists' adaptation of the random-association parlor game 'consequences': the head, the torso and the lower-half of the body have the appearance of being composed randomly, yet at the same time seamlessly – a wonderful coincidence, as it were.

Another kind of work by Sawada is more idyllic or nostalgic in tone. *eat [i : t] 1* consists of an image of the wall of a stone-built house which serves as a background to a lotus-filled pond; it could almost be the view from the terrace of a rural French restaurant. This view is outlined by a frame which opens up on the upper right-hand side, allowing the elegant floating silverware access to the image. The place exudes a nostalgic, sentimental, and almost quaint European atmosphere, and the fact that the title of the piece is an English word together with phonetic instructions on how to pronounce it (as in a tourist guidebook), suggests perhaps that it is the European dream itself that is good enough to eat. In spite of the invitation, however, one wonders about the window with its iron bars: could it be that we are excluded from the interior of this experience? *eat [i : t] 2,* on the other hand, presents an image of a blond-haired woman, her eyes invisible, her body treated relatively demurely, and with some difficult-to-interpret paperwork affixed. Is this also a European dream we are being invited to eat – but possibly another pleasure from which we may in fact be excluded?

generous time 1

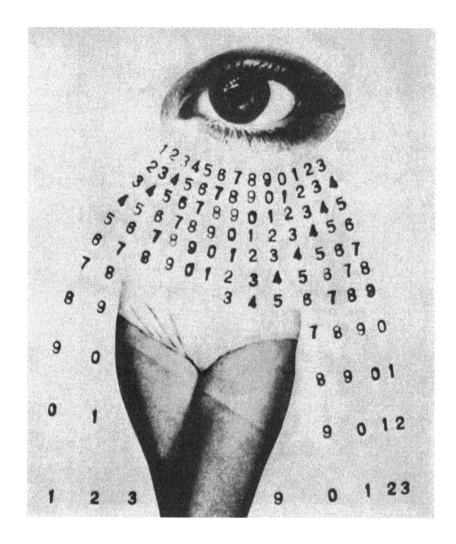

generous time 2

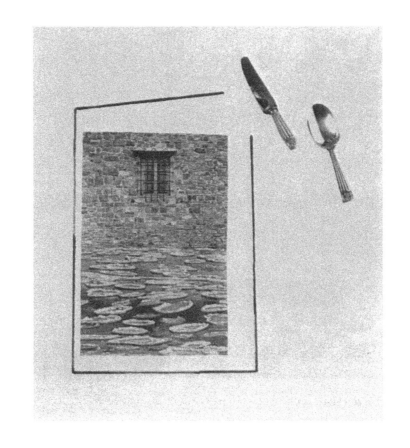

eat [i : t] l

eat [i : t] 2

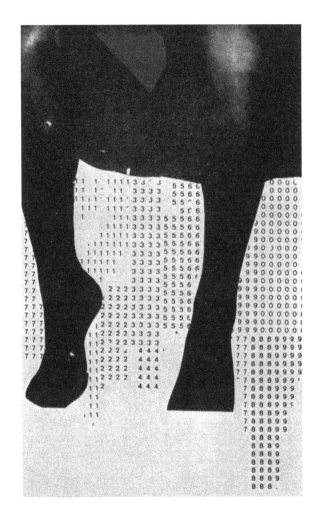

en chiffre – 2

SEKI Shiro (TANABE Shin)

Tanabe Shin was born in 1946 in Kyoto. From 1973 to 1978 he was a member of the VOU group under the name Seki Shiro. From 1979 to 1993, he was associated with the magazine *O*, edited by Tsuji Setsuko, and then in 1994 he founded the international little magazine, δ (*Delta*), which he described as 'a magnetic field for new (avant-garde) poetry which illuminates and changes from inside the world.' In Japan, he has had his work published in the catalog of the *Japanese and German Visual Poetry* exhibition held in Kitakami in 1999, and in separate issues of *Gendaishitecho* on visual poetry and Kitasono Katue; more recently, *Tokyo Poetry Journal* published his lexical poem, 'Midair Zipper', translated by John Solt, in a special issue featuring Butoh dance and Japanese modernism (2018). His work has been and continues to be shown at an impressive number of venues in Europe, notably at the *Japanese Visual Poetry* exhibit in Hamburg, Germany, in 1997, and at *Poésie Visuelle Japonaise (première exposition)* in Paris in 1998. In 2021 he is showing at *poésie visuelle internationale, les nouveaux ambassadeurs* in La Ciotat, France.

As Karl Young noted, women did not suffer from any chauvinistic editorial tendencies at the VOU Club, nor did Kitasono deny pages to overseas visual poets. In fact, *VOU* enthusiastically opened its print space to an array of foreign artists such as Pierre Garnier, Jean-Francoise Bory, Julien Blaine, Maurizio Nanucci, Sarenco, and Eugenio Miccini. The interactions were so robust that these European contributors attended *VOU* Club exhibitions in Tokyo. Tanabe as an editor continues to publish foreign work in his own δ to a remarkable degree.

The breadth of styles and methods Tanabe has pursued runs the gamut from works with a geometric yet primitive, outsider-art feel (*Poème ligné: un voyant*); an abstract painterly mode (*poème peint: un songe d'un polyèdre*), including a rare touch of cursive script; or the stripped down, elegant simplicity of *photopoem: a first man*, given a Bauhaus treatment. Works in the angular *parole sans parole* series focus on highlighting letters bereft of context – so much so that they appear as abstract art – while the mysterious *plastic poem: absence et image* provokes the question of what the relationship is between the identically shaped images of the approaching train and of the void. On the other hand, *plastic poem: portrait de <H. I.>*, with its monochrome setting, appears to be Cubist in nature, or like the camouflage design which developed from Cubist procedures. The last two images, the only ones not archived from *VOU*, are *plastic poem: un lettre de M. X.* and *poème plastique:* 市場の中の孤独 ('solitude inside the city market'). Both of these are spare and linear in style and have a subtle humor, whether in the dark silhouette of Monsieur X haunting his envelope, or in the attractive minimalism of the figure viewing the dark square where four lines meet like city streets converging on a marketplace.

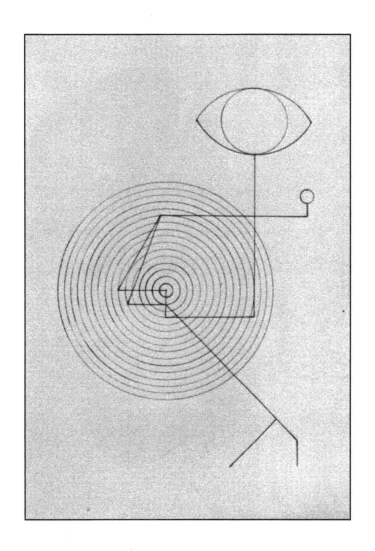

Poème ligné: un voyant

poème peint: un songe d'un polyèdre

photopoem: a first man

plastic poem: parole sans parole b-2

plastic poem: parole sans parole b-3

plastic poem : absence et image

plastic poem : portrait de <H. I.>

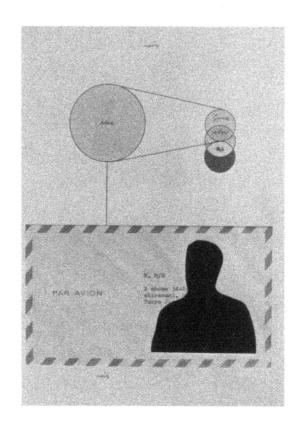

plastic poem: un lettre de M. X.

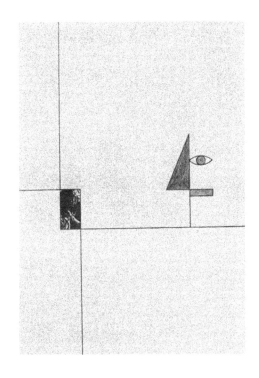

poéme plastique 市場の中の孤独

(solitude inside the city market)

TAKAHASHI Shōhachirō

Takahashi Shōhachirō (1933–2014), like Itō Motoyuki, was born in Kitakami City in the north of Japan. He was a member of the VOU Club from issue no. 55 until no. 160, the final issue in 1978. He was later associated with the poetry magazine *gui*, founded in 1979, and also the journal *Sei-en*. He had a long history of presenting his work in international contexts. For example, in the single year of 1968, he showed work, along with some VOU colleagues, at the *Characters on the Wall* exhibit in Modena, Italy, at the show *K1149000000* in Ferrara, Italy, and at the *First German Visual Poetry Exhibit* in Münster. Later, in 1990, Takahashi participated in a joint exhibit at the Ben Maltz Gallery in Los Angeles with British concrete poet Ian Hamilton Finlay. In 1995 Takahashi took part in a visual poetry debate at Yale and in the same year exhibited at the Yenchin Library at Harvard. *Renshi 2000–02*, a German and Japanese linked visual poetry work by Takahashi, Fujitomi Yasuo, Itō Motoyuki, Uemura Hiroo, and Klaus Peter Denker, the German visual poet and film-maker, was published by Hybriden-Verlag, Berlin, in 2002; in the following year he participated in the exhibition *Artword* with Dick Higgins at the Museum of Modern and Contemporary Art of Bolzano, Italy.

In 1958, by invitation of the de Campos brothers of the Noigrandes concrete poetry group in Brazil, Kitasono published 'Monotonous Space,' consisting largely of the austerely repetitive use of kanji combined with the hiragana symbol pronounced *no*, representing the possessive 'of.' Takahashi, who had joined the VOU group the year before, witnessed the success of 'Monotonous Space,' but, unlike many VOU members, Takahashi never imitated Kitasono, opting instead for his original muse. When he composed pieces evoking concrete, such as *bird 1* and *bird 2*, the viewer – especially in the latter case – is caught in a delirious swoon of movement and good humor. The work remains animatedly accessible, as if the viewer is drawn into the swarm to join the flock to become the ideogram for bird.

There is an openness in Takahashi's work inviting the viewer to participate. The *poesie animation* pieces – which have the subtitle *ai no kuni* (country of love) – are other examples. The first one, set upon a rock, brings to mind an epic version of the origami finger game, and, being set outside, one might imagine a picnic and humorous, offbeat results. The second one included here shows a large object thrown from a building top. This brings to mind those Fluxus performances which make the audience a key component in bringing the compositions to life; it is no coincidence that Takahashi took part in exhibits with Fluxus artists Shiomi Mieko and Dick Higgins. *block poem for endless <A>* and *<B>* remind me of a photo (see page 5) of the late Karl Young – to whom this book is dedicated – interacting with a Takahashi-like work: I think Karl and Shōhachirō would have been fast friends.

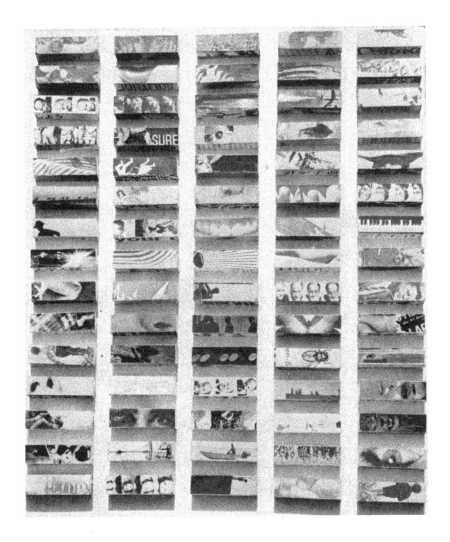

block poem c.

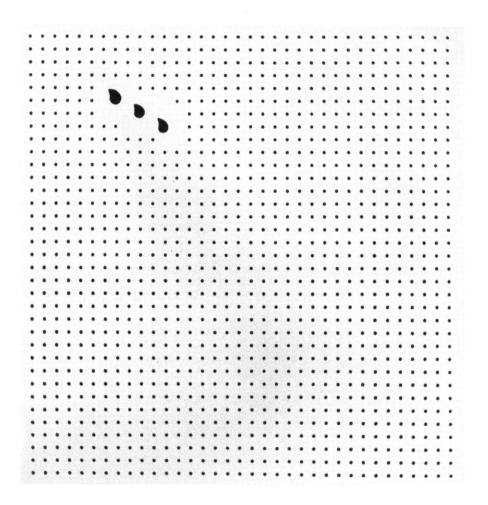

鳥 - I [bird]

鳥 - 2 [bird]

影 [shadow]

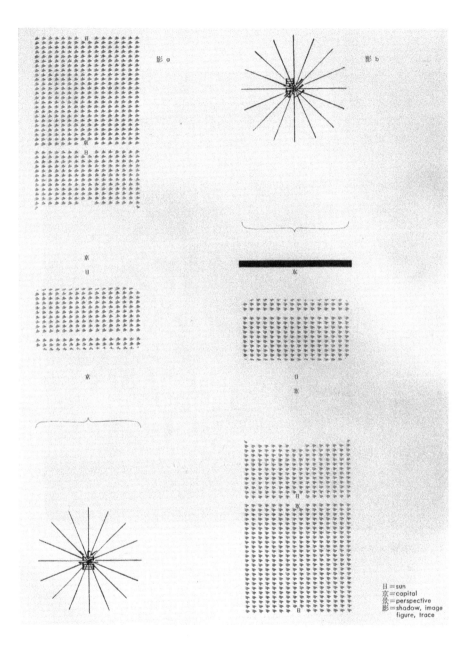

影 a

影 b

日 = sun
京 = capital
景 = perspective
影 = shadow, image
    figure, trace

90

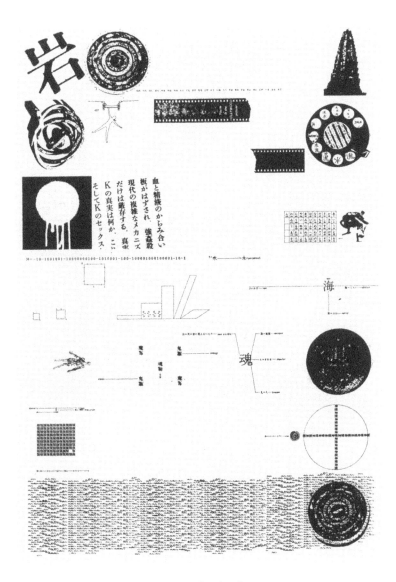

water-land fire-land a

poesie animation (ai no kuni)

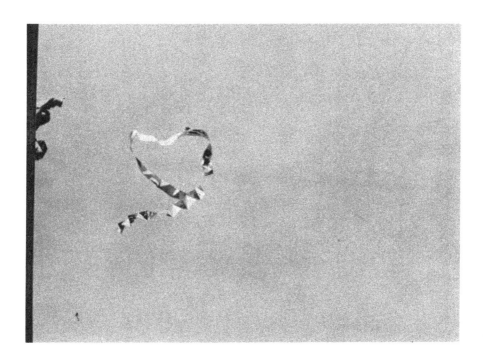

poesie animation (ai no kuni)

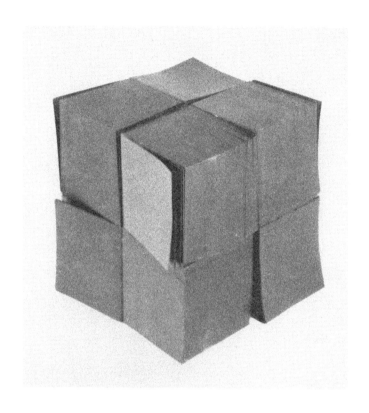

block poem for endless <A>

block poem for endless <B>

HIBINO Fumiko

Almost nothing is known about Hibino Fumiko, except that she was a prolific contributor of images to *VOU*. Even her methods of working are not well-understood although they may have been influenced by the cameraless photography technique – involving placing objects directly onto light-sensitive paper – developed by Christian Schad (Schadographs), Laszlo Moholy-Nagy (photograms), and Man Ray (rayographs) in Europe in 1918–22. Karl Young, one of the original editors of this book before his death in 2017, regarded her work highly; reprinted here from his *Light and Dust Anthology of Poetry* is his introduction to her work, 'Questions of Light: Selected Plastic Poems of Hibino Fumiko.'

Hibino Fumiko was a member of the Japanese VOU group, founded by Kitasono Katue. One of the practices of the group, as described by Kitasono in his 1966 essay 'A Note On Plastic Poetry' is that 'Poetry started with a quill pen, and should come to an end with a ball-point pen.... The camera is fit to be used expressively by poets.' He and his group went on to produce 'Plastic Poems,' that is, poems composed of photographs. Kitasono's poems sometimes included text, but always in the Roman alphabet and in English or French; he never used Japanese script in his plastic poems. With a few exceptions, the members of the VOU group avoided language as previously understood. Instead, they sought a new iconography and syntax made from photographs. The objects photographed and their treatment after exposure covered a huge spectrum, particularly given the resources available to them. In my introduction to Kitasono's major selection of poems translated into English (Kitasono, trans. Solt, 2007), I suggested that this practice foreshadowed the photographic base of the World Wide Web, and specifically the photo poetry created for it, or with tools related to it.

Hibino Fumiko was one of the members of the group who took the process to one of its extremes. Her primary work consisted of photographs of light itself. This examination of the basic means by which we see and the medium that allows photographs to be made took her through a remarkable body of work. Like many women in new media, she was not restricted by male dominance of previous art forms, particularly in the relatively free environment of the VOU group, where she published some of her work. That's about all I or anyone I can find can say for sure about her. John Solt, Kitasono's translator, and his and my friends and colleagues in Japan, including other members of the VOU group, know little about her. The addresses they have found have not yielded responses other than stamps from the post office reading 'No longer at this address,' or something similar. Several poets who went to the address where she lived while an active member of the VOU group were able to learn nothing from people living in the neighborhood.... She should certainly be included in collections of VOU group members in the future.

moving light 7 —750714

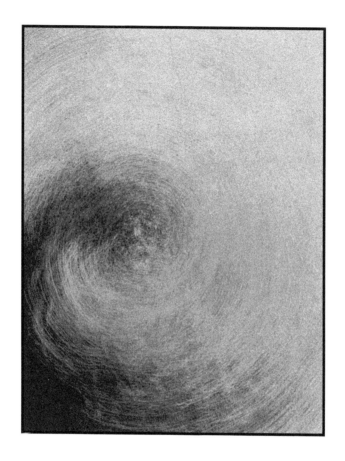

turn light 9 −750924

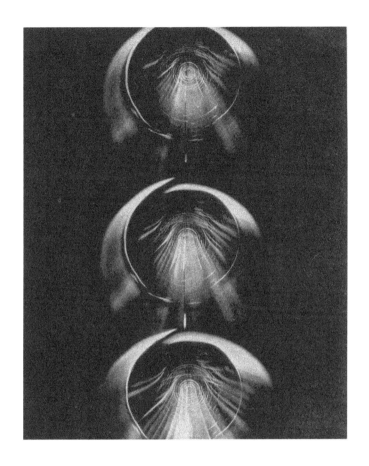

negative light 15 –76131

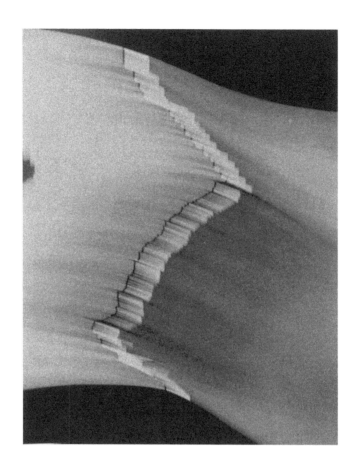

negative light 16 –76131

pictograph [C] 20, 76255

pictograph [Y] 19, 76255

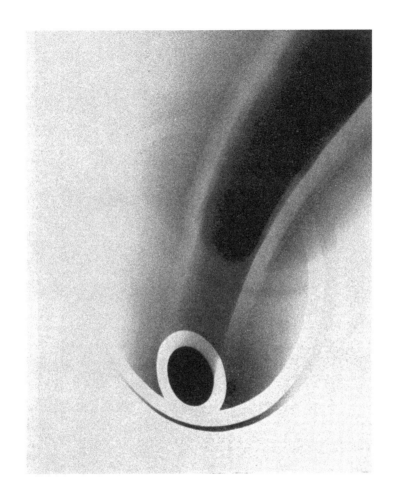

down 21, 76328

GLIMMER 19770901

swing light 32 77316

77

SEPTEMBRE-OCTOBRE 1960

AFTERWORD

My Intro to Vispoe

When I think about the early days of this project, I am carried back twenty years to my former apartment in the Itabashi area of Tokyo, where I was working on my article 'The Literary Avant-Garde in Japan: VOU Research Notes,' later published in the December 2001 issue of the *Hitotsubashi University Journal of Arts and Sciences*. The editorial staff of this university journal did superlative layout work, with the photographic paper they used showing the visual poems from the VOU Club I had chosen to their best advantage. I sent offprints of that article to people featured in it, notably Tanabe Shin, Takahashi Shōhachirō and John Solt, and was pleased with the praise it received; this was an important moment in the story of my commitment to the work of the VOU Club.

Visual poetry and Japanese avant-garde poetry had initially caught my eye during the time when I was coediting a Tokyo-based literary journal, *Printed Matter: Japan's International Review of Literature and the Arts*. While doing this, I came across a series of broadsides brought out, with the cooperation of an American editor living in the Kanto area, by Karl Young's Light and Dust Press in Kenosha, Wisconsin; the series, called Word / Light Pescia, published 'the work of contemporary Japanese visual poets,' including Tanabu Hiroshi and Kamimura Hiroo. Soon after, I came across a visual work by Portuguese visual poet Fernando Aguiar featuring a forefinger and thumb framing a spray of alphabetic letters; this so caught my eye that we used it on the cover of the next issue of the magazine.

More or less concurrently, John Solt was submitting, and we were publishing, his translations of Kitasono Katue, so that I was in the fortunate position of being a part of the expansion and reformation of how Japanese poetry was perceived by English-speaking audiences. Myself, I hadn't yet fully realized that there was much more to poetry in Japan than haiku or tanka, but encountering Solt's translations in real time as they appeared began to chip away at my preconceptions. What crystallized my literary awakening to a wider range of contemporary Japanese poetry and art was the publication of Solt's *Shredding the Tapestry of Meaning: The Poetry and Poetics of Kitasono Katue (1902–1978)*, a book that created a major breakthrough – and not only for me – in western understanding of Japanese avant-garde writing in both the prewar and postwar periods.

From this point on, it became an obsession of mine to find copies of *VOU* and to attend Kit Kat events ('Kit Kat' being the name Ezra Pound had given to Kitasono) around Tokyo. In the late 1990s and early 2000s I penned a monthly column in the *Japan Times*, called Poetry Mignette, and for one of these instalments, I interviewed the visual poet Nakamura Keiichi. Soon after this, at an exhibit at Gallery Oculus, in Shinagawa, Tokyo, I learned that there was another small gallery at the Keiyudoh bookstore, where I was flabbergasted to find a few dozen copies of *VOU* for sale rather cheaply. It turned out that the owner of the bookstore, Sugimoto Teruo, had been a colleague of Yoda Yoshiharu, another VOU visual and lexical poet (whose work, although not included here, also deserves attention). This find and my fascination with the work made me want to put together an anthology, and Karl Young, as scholar, editor and poet, perfectly matched the project. Karl agreed and we discussed how to progress.

It was then that I reached out to Takahashi Shōhachirō, who kindly and gracefully allowed me to purchase another two dozen or so issues of *VOU* from him, so that I now had enough copies to give me confidence to go through with the project. (He also recommended that Itō Motoyuki's work should be included in the anthology and received permission from him for that to happen.) In 2004, Sugimoto, the Keiyudoh proprietor, published an issue of his elegant journal *Le Carrosse d'Or* which included a facsimile of my hand-written prose poem, 'Postmodern Transcendentalist: Takahashi Shōhachirō,' while in the same year Takahashi exhibited his own work at the Keiyudoh bookstore. The exhibition featured his 'capsule' works where he asked many people to contribute words and images to be sealed in jars, a procedure quite indicative of Itō's way of doing things. (See *capsule plan 3* on page 46 for an example of this kind of work by Itō.) It was my first (and possibly last) effort as a visual poet. Neither Solt nor I remember what our actual works consisted of, but I do remember meeting Takahashi with his oxygen tank in tow; I doubt it was nitrous oxide, though the atmosphere felt jolly. As a final note to my vispoe upbringings, my virgin book of poems, *Japlish Whiplash* (Printed Matter Press, 2010) included homages to Okazaki Katsuhiko, Takahashi Shōhachirō, Tsuji Setsuko and Shimizu Toshihiko, with their respective visual works on facing pages.

On the Vispoe Book Beginnings

Karl's original concept for the anthology, which I thought was too complicated, was to carry the whole volume on his online site, as well as publish it both on CD-ROM and as a physical book. Nevertheless, being young and full of confidence, I agreed with the plan saying I would pay the printing costs of the physical book, which would be published by his Light and Dust books imprint. Surfing the wave of my rather naïve, idealistic exuberance, I sent the whole collection of magazines, along with two larger VOU anthologies, to Karl. He then impressed by creating a sequestered online site highlighting three or four VOU visual poets. I had hoped that he would go on to update the site with the work of other poets, but he didn't. I am not sure why he was reluctant to post more, but I think partly he was frustrated at not being able to contact the photographer whose work he especially admired, Hibino Fumiko. (His short article about her is reprinted here on the opening page of the section devoted to her work.) He may have also wanted me to commit more by fronting funds towards the project. So, with book production seemingly in perpetual hiatus, I dedicated more than ten years to translating the complete poems of another VOU poet, Torii Shōzō.

Every now and then I would try to contact Karl, sometimes through John Solt in wishing a happy birthday and so on, but we weren't able to connect or continue with the book. I felt it was my fault for not keeping in touch more – but Karl also had physical issues to deal with. John joked to me that I would never see those copies of *VOU* again. But, even as *Printed Matter* faded and poetry journals were becoming defunct at a furious pace, I had the honor of being asked to join the editorial staff of a new journal we call *ToPoJo (Tokyo Poetry Journal)*, founded because we love the feel of papyrus, because there are still many talented poets in and around Tokyo, and because there is still much Japanese avant-garde poetry and art needing to be introduced to the world and *ToPoJo* is a channel for that.

I thus had the opportunity of editing a special issue on Japan and the Beats in 2015. During the production of this, we received news from Karl Young's Kanto-based cousin Kris Kondo that Karl had died. Not only that, but there was a specific request from Karl: 'An intermediate work is the *VOU: Surrealism's Esperantic Permutations* anthology I have been editing with Taylor Mignon. Should I die in the surgery of this month, Mr. Alexander has agreed to contact Mr. Mignon and make arrangements to publish the book as the last title under the Light and Dust imprint. Funding for the book has already been arranged with benefactors in Japan, and Mr. Mignon will be able to guide Mr. Alexander through its receipt.' Alas, no such funding had yet materialized, but Paul Rossiter at Isobar Press saved the day by picking up the baton. Karl's executors, Charles Alexander, Karl Kempton and Dan Waber graciously supported the cause and miraculously most of the issues and books were returned to me, thus resuscitating this project. *Surrealism's Esperantic Permutations* was the original title: at the time I had been thinking that the VOU visual poetry combination of French, English and different types of Japanese syllabary, in different sizes and forms, along with collage-like images, was like coining a new (unspoken) language, with everything morphing beyond Esperanto – and, of course, the surrealism of the VOU group was idiosyncratic in spite of its European instigation. But now it seemed best to drop the original, possibly idiosyncratic, title in favor of the current, more strictly informative one. The result is this book.

Influence on Coterie Journals from 1979: The *VOU* Effect

After Kitasono died in 1978, the VOU Club disbanded and the *VOU* magazine ceased publication. However, those who had been engaged with VOU went on to found new coteries and new magazines, thus transmitting and perpetuating Kitasono's legacy and opening up spaces for further avant-garde creativity. A leading magazine of this type is *gui*, edited by poet, folk guitarist and jazz trumpeter (and founder of a social club for visiting hot springs) Okunari Tatsu (1942–2015), the last poet to join the VOU Club in 1978. Okunari wrote a column for *gui* called *Ai gotto rizumu* (I got rhythm), in which he often discussed Kitasono while in issue #107 he wrote about the history of Japanese jazz. The most notable continuation of the VOU impulse in *gui* was that Takahashi Shōhachirō's visual poems / designs were adopted for the covers in quite a lengthy succession of issues. For example, #107 interestingly sported Takahashi's 第一話の黒箱 (or *Part 1 talk of the black box*) on the front cover (in the West, the back cover) while the back cover reversed the image and the letters and numbers of the journal's title. (It should be noted that this 2016 issue was a special memorial issue for Okunari Tatsu and contains John Solt's obituary for him.) Solt, who has been a member of *gui* for over thirty years, recently published a book gathering his poems published in the group's journal in a large-sized (nearly 700 pages), bilingual volume of poetry under the title, *Poems for the Unborn* 「生まれぬ者への詩」 (Shichosha, 2020). The *gui* coterie, publishing three times a year, also gathers at a 'snack bar' in Ginza for social get-togethers; in Japan, contributors must pay to join a coterie and print in its organ's pages, and *gui* is the most expensive.

Another major handing-on of the VOU flame was initiated when Tsuji Setsuko founded (in 1979) the quarterly *0*, which she thereafter edited until her death in 1993. Among my modest collection of post-VOU related journals, this is the one which most strictly and astonishingly follows the aesthetics of *VOU* as far as cover, contents pages and even the contents themselves are concerned; in style it adheres to a simple format, crisp and clean. I discovered an almost complete set of this journal towards the end of the making of this book; if I had had the series before I had started the project with Karl, this book might have looked very different. Like *VOU, 0* wasn't all about poetry but also contained essays on art and criticism, and 'musique,' or experimental musical notations. *0* was also open to foreign submissions, publishing, for example, American visual poet Scott Helmes' provocative visual poetry.

Following on from *0*, δ (*delta*) was led by Tanabe Shin (VOU nom de plume, Seki Shiro, the name he appears under in this anthology), another member of the generation who, like Okunari, joined the VOU Club shortly before Kitasono's death. Tanabe contributed to *0* during its existence, and then started publishing δ in 1993, after Tsuji had died, thus forming a seamless line of VOU-influenced journals, running from the foundation of *O* in 1979 through to the present day. Sawada Shin'ichi contributed to δ but stopped submitting work in around 2007, leaving speculation as to his status: even Tanabe, the editor of δ, could not provide information about him. What is especially noteworthy about δ is that it continues *VOU's* editorial policy of publishing the works of overseas artist-poets, including some from the *VOU* era, such as Julien Blaine, and others who would likely have been published there if it had continued longer. It also publishes younger visual poets who carry forward Kitasono's 'plastic' impulse, for example, Yarita Misako and Kikuchi Hajime.

Another line of descent begins with Iwamoto Shūzō. Iwamoto and Kitasono had collaborated on three journals: *VOU, Madame Blanche* and *Hakushi* (Blank Paper), but then, after splitting with Kitasono, Iwamoto founded his own coterie, Cénacle de Pan Poésie; the next step was when Kawamura Yoichi, who had been a member of Pan Poésie, started his own circle, Sei-en. The journal of this circle, *Sei-en* (Blue Flame) was later edited by Shima Yufuko and then, after Shima's death, by Yarita Misako. The journal is still ongoing; it regularly featured works by Takahashi Shōhachirō and runs a column by former VOU member, poet Shiraishi Kazuko (1931–); Solt's lexical works accompanying Takahashi's visual works were a regular collaborative feature of the magazine. Thus the link goes from Kitasono to Iwamoto to Kawamura and so to the younger generation. *Sei-en* is inexpensive to produce because the issues are printed at a prison in Fuchū. When I met *gui* editor Okunari at a party, I told him I was also a member of Sei-en and he stuck out his hand and said *sei-en*, which is a homophone of 1,000 yen, pointing fun at the relative low coterie member rates.

Finally, by far the most elegant of the post-Kitasono modernistic, coterie journals, was Torii Shōzō's *TRAP*. Uniquely, it moved away from stapler binding to high-quality, hand-folded *washi*, or Japanese paper, and used letterpress printing; the magazine was loose leaf with the rough outer edges of a natural paper, and copies of the photos were hand-glued onto the pages. Eric Selland has commented well on these production values: 'It is quite impressive that a small, underground magazine would go to such lengths in the beauty of its design and the attention to the materials used. It is a reflection of their attention to the materiality of language, such that the poem, as well as its medium – the small magazine – has its own physicality and is also a work of art. The hand-made paper itself is already a work of art before its use in the printing of the magazine. This is one of the interesting characteristics of Japan's avant-garde in that there is a desire to retain some element of tradition and beauty, whereas the American avant-garde has generally rejected anything smacking of traditional aesthetics, often preferring stapled sheets of mimeographed pages in a concern with content alone' (personal communication, November 5, 2021). Among the VOU Club members whose visual work was featured in *TRAP* were Kitasono, surrealist photographer Yamamoto Kansuke, Okazaki Katsuhiko (who also penned essays on new art) and lexical work by poets Shirashi Kazuko, Kuroda Iri and Takahashi. In addition to all this small-press activity, *Gendaishitecho*, Japan's most established poetry magazine has published specially themed issues on Visual Poetry, such as the one in April 2000, which printed Takahashi, Solt and Tanabe; also included were Niikuni Seiichi and Fujitomi Yasuo.

After Afterword

Revisiting this project and seeing it through to completion is most satisfying. Every time I view these works, I am intrigued and discover a new element or idea. If this book is able to help rectify the stereotype that Japanese poetry is essentially haiku, then I would be pleased. Jean Francois Bory will come out with a book on Kitasono in French later this year, and Nancy Perloff, curator of modern and contemporary collections at the Getty Research Institute, has written a major book on concrete poetry, including discussions of Kitasono and Niikuni, which will come out in early 2022. I hope this book on the VOU visual poets of the 1960s and 1970s may contribute to this strengthening wave of interest in an often overlooked aspect of twentieth-century and contemporary Japanese art and poetry.

Taylor Mignon, October 27, 2021

Kitasono Katue at the Japan Dental College in 1977, in his office with his administrative assistant, Tsuji Setsuko.

ACKNOWLEDGEMENTS

This book is dedicated to the lasting influence of prime mover Kitasono Katue and pioneering poet and editor Karl Young. I would also like to express my warm thanks to my daughter Ryuka, whose company during this time lifted my spirits; to Kris Kondo, without whose help this project would never have been revived; to Charles Alexander, director of Chax Press, visual poet Karl Kempton, and poet-editor Dan Waber, who were essential in gaining permission from Karl's estate to proceed with the project in Japan; to Nakamura Keiichi, who assisted me in the beginning of this project with advice; to Noda Naotoshi (Japan's leading critic of Kitasono Katue) for his scholarship; to Mōri Ichiro for securing permission from the Kitasono estate to reproduce editorial material from *VOU* magazine; to Zoria Petkoska and Barbara Summerhawk, who offered comments on the works of Okazaki Katsuhiko; to Jeffrey Johnson, who assisted with the choices of Hibino Fumiko's photos and helped to organize the manuscript; to Katō Jin ('Bibliophile Drummer') for key assistance in tracking down information about the contributors; to Ben Swift for finding and supplying some extra Tsuji Setsuko images; to Tanabe Shin, whose kind correspondence offered a wealth of biographical information not only about himself but about others featured in this book; and especially to John Solt for putting up with my queries regarding the project overall and for generously offering relevant information; without his scholarship, this book would not have been conceived. My thanks also go to Eric Selland, who agreed to help with this in spite of his own busy schedule, and to Isobar publisher Paul Rossiter, whose sharp, steady guidance throughout the whole process was key in making this realizable.

IMAGE SOURCES

TSUJI Setsuko

high summer	*VOU* 119, 1969, p. 20
Photo poem	*VOU* 129, 1971, p. 18
op. 4	*VOU* 142, 1974, p. 21
op. 5	*VOU* 143, 1974, p. 27
op. 5	*VOU* 146, 1975, p. 22
op 77-1	*VOU* 154, 1977, p. 24
opus 1	*VOU* 159, 1978, p. 17
op. 1	*O* 1, 1979, p. 15
drome	*O* 11, 1981, p. 15
op. 001 or 川のある記憶	*O* 23, 1983, p. 14
two people eating the moon	*O* 27, 1986, p. 15
op. 016	*O* 30, 1987, p. 13
op. 017	*O* 31, 1987, p. 15

SHIMIZU Toshihiko

high noon	*VOU* 62, 1958, p. 18
text picture	*VOU* 99, 1965, p. 26
letter picture A2	*VOU* 100, 1965, p. 20
letter picture B1	*VOU* 100, 1965, p. 21
hommage a augusto de campos: popcrete poem	*VOU* 115, 1968, p. 17
variation	*VOU* 116, 1968, p. 22
op. 691	*VOU* 118, 1969, p. 23
sculpture in environment	*VOU* 119, 1969, p. 26
anti-illusion 1	*VOU* 128, 1971, p. 22
anti-illusion 2	*VOU* 128, 1971, p. 23
postcard event / sky	*VOU* 147, 1975, p. 21

ITŌ Motoyuki

inversion c	*VOU* 97, 1964, p. 18
inversion d	*VOU* 97, 1964, p. 19
inversion e	*VOU* 100, 1965, p. 24

capsule plan 3	*VOU* 110, 1967, p. 25
plastic poem 11	*VOU* 122, 1970, p. 2
耳の祭 *a (ear festival a, b, c)*	*VOU* 126, 1971, pp. 24–25

OKAZAKI Katsuhiko

♀ *and* ♀	*VOU* 118, 1969, p. 26
summer letter 1	*VOU* 128, 1971, p. 24
chaos	*VOU* 132, 1972, p. 21
lovely vomit 4	*VOU* 136, 1973, p. 18
adam & eve	*VOU* 147, 1975, p. 18
poemgraphy 3	*VOU* 150, 1976, p. 26
poemgraphy <requiem to A>	*VOU* 157, 1977, p. 26
poemgraphy <requiem to Z>	*VOU* 157, 1977, p. 27
poemgraphy: requiem by the rain	*VOU* 158, 1977, p. 20

KIYOHARA Etsushi

op. 6001	*VOU* 77, 1960, p. 20
composition e	*VOU* 87, 1963, p. 24
op. 1	*VOU* 118, 1969, p. 20
op. −70−A−018	*VOU* 130, 1972, p. 20
op. −74−A−79	*VOU* 144, 1975, p. 22
op. −74−A−80	*VOU* 144, 1975, p. 23
op. −75−A−151	*VOU* 148, 1975, p. 24
op. −76−A−153	*VOU* 150, 1976, p. 22
op. −76−A−160	*VOU* 153, 1976, p. 21

SAWADA Shin'ichi

generous time 1	*VOU* 143, 1974, p. 20
generous time 2	*VOU* 144, 1974, p. 24
eat [i : t] 1	*VOU* 147, 1975, p. 19
eat [i : t] 2	*VOU* 148, 1975, p. 20
en chiffre − 2	*VOU* 152, 1976, p. 19

SEKI Shiro (TANABE Shin)

Poème ligné: un voyant	*VOU* 151, 1976, p. 19
poème peint: un songe d'un polyèdre	*VOU* 152, 1976, p. 23
photopoem: a first man	*VOU* 153, 1976, p. 23
plastic poem: parole sans parole b-2	*VOU* 157, 1977, p. 20
plastic poem: parole sans parole b-3	*VOU* 157, 1977, p. 21
plastic poem: absence et image	*VOU* 158, 1977, p. 21
plastic poem: portrait de <H. I.>	*VOU* 159, 1978, p.19
plastic poem: un lettre de M. X.	*O* 5, 1979, p.19
poéme plastique 市場の中の孤独	*O* 29, 1987, p.15

TAKAHASHI Shōhachirō

block poem c.	*VOU* 110, 1967, pp. 23–24
鳥 – 1 *(bird)*	*VOU* 115, 1968, p. 20
鳥 – 2 *(bird)*	*VOU* 115, 1968, p. 21
影 *(shadow)*	*VOU* 118, 1969, p. 21
water-land fire-land a	*VOU* 122, 1970, p. 24
poesie animation (ai no kuni)	*VOU* 132, 1972, p. 26
poesie animation (ai no kuni)	*VOU* 132, 1972, p. 27
block poem for endless <A>	*VOU* 136, 1973, p. 20
block poem for endless <B>	*VOU* 136, 1973, p. 21

HIBINO Fumiko

moving light 7 –750714	*VOU* 147, 1975, p. 26
turn light 9 –750924	*VOU* 148, 1975, p. 26
negative light 15 –76131	*VOU* 151, 1976, p. 22
negative light 16 –76131	*VOU* 151, 1976, p. 23
pictograph [C] 20, 76255	*VOU* 153, 1976, p. 18
pictograph [Y] 19, 76255	*VOU* 153, 1976, p. 19
down 21, 76328	*VOU* 154, 1977, p. 20
GLIMMER 19770901	*VOU* 158, 1977, p. 25
swing light 32 77316	*VOU* 159, 1978, p. 27

BIBLIOGRAPHY

Bohn, Willard, *The Aesthetics of Visual Poetry: 1914-1928,* (Chicago: The University of Chicago Press, 1986).

Broinowski, Adam, *Cultural Responses to Occupation in Japan: The Performing Body During and After the Cold War* (London: Bloomsbury Academic, 2016).

Hirato Renkichi, *Spiral Staircase: Collected Poems,* translated by Sho Sugita, Ugly Duckling Press (2017).

Igarashi Yoshikuni, *Bodies of Memory: Narratives of War in Postwar Japanese Culture, 1945-1970* (Princeton: Princeton University Press, 2000).

Jackson, K. David, Eric Vos & Johanna Drucker (eds.), *Experimental – Visual – Concrete: Avant Garde Critical Studies Since the 1960s* (Amsterdam: Rodopi, 1996).

Johnson, Jeffrey, *Haiku Poetics in Twentieth-Century Avant-Garde Poetry* (Lanham, MD: Lexington Books, 2011).

Kitasono Katue, *Oceans Beyond Monotonous Space: Selected Poems*, trans. John Solt, introduction by Karl Young (Hollywood, CA: highmoonoon, 2007).

Mignon, Taylor, 'The Literary Avant-Garde in Japan: VOU Research Notes', *Hitotsubashi Journal of Arts and Sciences,* 42/1, 59-80, 2001.

Okunari Tatsu, *Sea of Hats: Poems and Drawings*, trans. John Solt (Tokyo: Momoko Press, 1988).

Ridgely, Steven C., *Japanese Counterculture: The Antiestablishment Art of Terayama Shuji* (Minneapolis: The University of Minnesota Press, 2011).

Sas, Miryam, *Fault Lines: Cultural Memory and Japanese Surrealism* (Stanford, CA: Stanford University Press, 1999).

———, *Experimental Arts in Postwar Japan: Moments of Encounter, Engagement, and Imagined Return* (Cambridge, MA: Harvard University Asia Center, 2011).

Silverberg, Miriam, *Erotic Grotesque Nonsense: The Mass Culture of Japanese Modern Times* (Berkeley, CA: University of California Press, 2006).

Slaymaker, Douglas N., *The Body in Postwar Japanese Fiction* (Abingdon-on-Thames: Routledge, 2004).

Solt, John, *Shredding the Tapestry of Meaning: The Poetry and Poetics of Kitasono Katue* (Cambridge, MA: Harvard University Asia Center, 1999).

Young, Karl, *Light & Dust Anthology of Poetry,* http://www.thing.net/~grist/l&d/lighthom.htm

BIOGRAPHIES

TAYLOR MIGNON is a poet, editor, translator and university lecturer living in Saitama. He teaches a Kenneth Rexroth seminar at Rikkyo University and Creative Writing at Keio and Musashi Universities. In *Kyoto Journal* 86, he is credited as someone who 'brings people together, creates events that showcase creativity and give rise to more creativity….' He coedited *Poesie Yaponesia: A Bilingual Anthology* (Printed Matter Press, 2000), coedited and cotranslated *Distant Frogs: Selected Senryu by Gengorō* (The Hokuseido Press, 2007), and led the translation and editing of *Bearded Cones & Pleasure Blades: The Collected Poems of Torii Shōzō* (highmoonoon, 2013). He is cofounding editor of *Tokyo Poetry Journal*, responsible for a special book-length issue on Japan and the Beats, and in 2017 for an issue on Butoh dance and Japanese modernism. His translations are slated to appear in an upcoming anthology of Japanese experimental poetry of the twentieth century (New Directions, 2022).

ERIC SELLAND is an American poet and translator living in Tokyo. He is the author of *Object States* (Theenk Books, 2018), *Beethoven's Dream* (Isobar Press, 2015), *Arc Tangent* (Isobar Press, 2013), *Still Lifes* (Hank's Original Loose Gravel Press, 2012), and *The Condition of Music* (Sink Press, 2000). His translation of *The Guest Cat*, a novel by Takashi Hiraide, was on the *New York Times* bestseller list in early 2014, and his translation of poems by Kiwao Nomura, *The Day Laid Bare*, was chosen as a Recommended Translation by The Poetry Book Society, UK, for their winter 2020 season. His most recently published book-length poetry translation is of *Kusudama* by Minoru Yoshioka (Isobar Press, 2021). Selland is co-editing an anthology of twentieth-century Japanese experimental poetry with poet and translator Sawako Nakayasu, which is scheduled to appear from New Directions Books in 2022. He makes his living as an independent translator of Japanese economic research reports.

NUMERO 97

29 ANNEE

BIMENSUEL

■

PRIX DE NUMERO:

JAPON:

ETRANGER: 4 Fr.

IMPRIMÉ EN JAPON

CPSIA information can be obtained
at www.ICGtesting.com
Printed in the USA
LVHW070029150222
711160LV00006B/70